GIVE THOSE NYMPHS SOME HOOTERS!

Doonesbury Books by G.B. Trudeau

In Large Format

A DOONESBURY BOOK
by G. B. TRUDEAU

GIVE THOSE NYMPHS SOME HOOTERS!

...THE ARRIVAL OF GERALDO WAS PERHAPS INEVITABLE.

PLEASE! I BEG YOU! DO NOT LET YOUR CHILDREN WATCH THIS!

B-B-B BRAT!

ANDREWS and McMEEL   A UNIVERSAL PRESS SYNDICATE COMPANY   KANSAS CITY • NEW YORK

DOONESBURY is syndicated internationally by Universal Press Syndicate.

Give Those Nymphs Some Hooters! copyright © 1989 by G.B. Trudeau. All rights reserved. Printed in the United States of America. No part of this book may be used or reproduced in any manner whatsoever without written permission except in the case of reprints in the context of reviews. For information, write Andrews and McMeel, a Universal Press Syndicate Company, 4900 Main Street, Kansas City, Missouri 64112.

ISBN: 0-8362-1858-2

Library of Congress Catalog Card Number: 89-84812

"Donald starts out each day talking to the doormen at the Trump Tower. The doormen love him. He is a man of the people."

—From Donald Trump's résumé

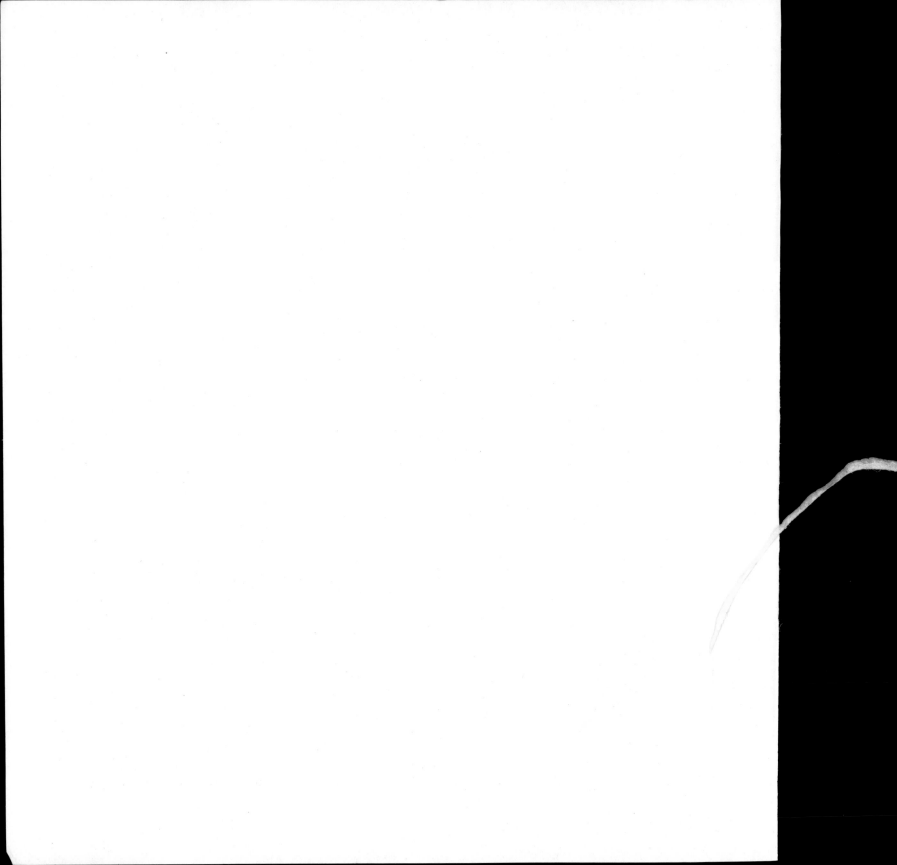

11

12

13

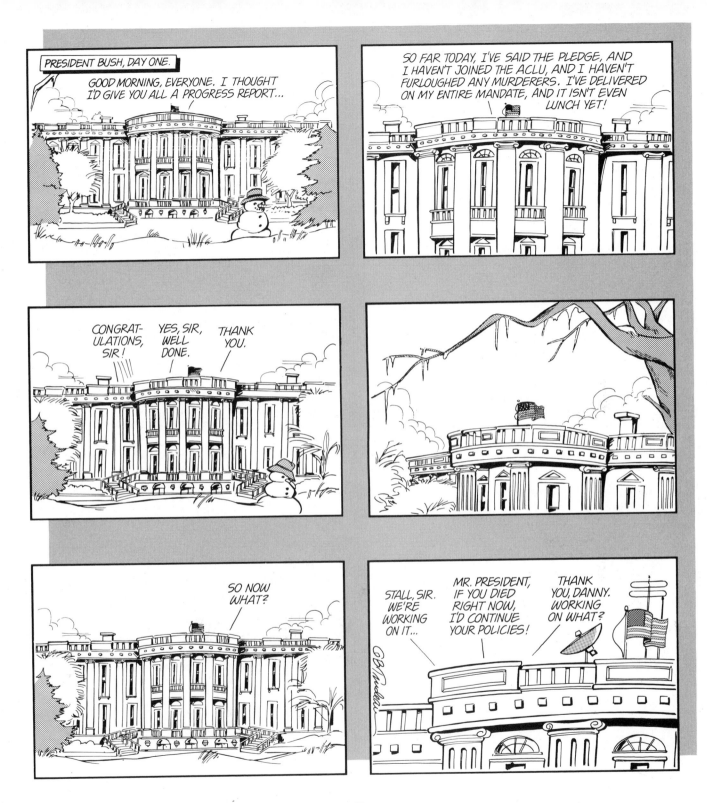

17

Panel 1: THE SOCIETY'S DISPLAY CASES, WHILE OVERCROWDED, ARE WIDELY CONCEDED TO HOLD THE WORLD'S FINEST PRIVATE COLLECTION OF SKULLS...

Panel 2: ...INCLUDING THOSE OF SOME OF HISTORY'S MOST ILLUSTRIOUS FIGURES, SUCH AS KIERKEGAARD, MADAME CURIE, NAPOLEON... — N. BONAPARTE

Panel 3: ...AND THE SOCIETY'S MOST PRIZED CATCH—TUTANKHAMEN, PINCHED BY A BOARD MEMBER OF THE METROPOLITAN MUSEUM OF ART. — TUTANKHAMEN

Panel 4: LESS WELL-KNOWN IS THE SOCIETY'S GAG COLLECTION... / HI! I'M DR. LIVINGSTONE! / HA, HA, HA! / STOP IT! YOU'RE KILLING US!

Panel 5: AN UNSUSPECTING PRESIDENT-ELECT ARRIVES FOR THE WINTER MEETING OF SKULL AND BONES. / POPPY, WE'VE GOT A LITTLE SURPRISE FOR YOU! / YOU DO?

Panel 6: IF YOU'LL JUST LOOK UP YONDER, RIGHT NEXT TO PANCHO VILLA, YOU SHOULD BE ABLE TO SPOT THE GLEAMING BRAINPAN OF THE EIGHTH PRESIDENT OF THE UNITED STATES! / WHAT?

Panel 7: YOU MEAN, YOU FELLOWS PINCHED THE SKULL OF MARTIN VAN BUREN JUST TO HONOR ME? I DON'T BELIEVE IT! THAT'S JUST SO THOUGHTFUL!

Panel 8: WELL, WE JUST FELT... WHAT ARE YOU DOING? / WRITING YOU GUYS A THANK-YOU NOTE!

Panel 9: THE PRESENTATION. / POPPY, IN YOUR HONOUR, WE HAVE ACQUIRED THE SKULL OF MARTIN VAN BUREN!

Panel 10: BESIDES BEING THE LAST SITTING VICE PRESIDENT TO BECOME PRESIDENT, VAN BUREN, LIKE YOU, WAS A MAN OF TREMENDOUS ACCOMPLISHMENTS, SUCH AS...

Panel 11: SUCH AS... UM...

Panel 12: WELL, ANYWAY, WE THOUGHT IT WAS REALLY APPROPRIATE. / IT IS! IT'S A NEAT CONNECTION, YOU GUYS!

27

33

34

42

45

47

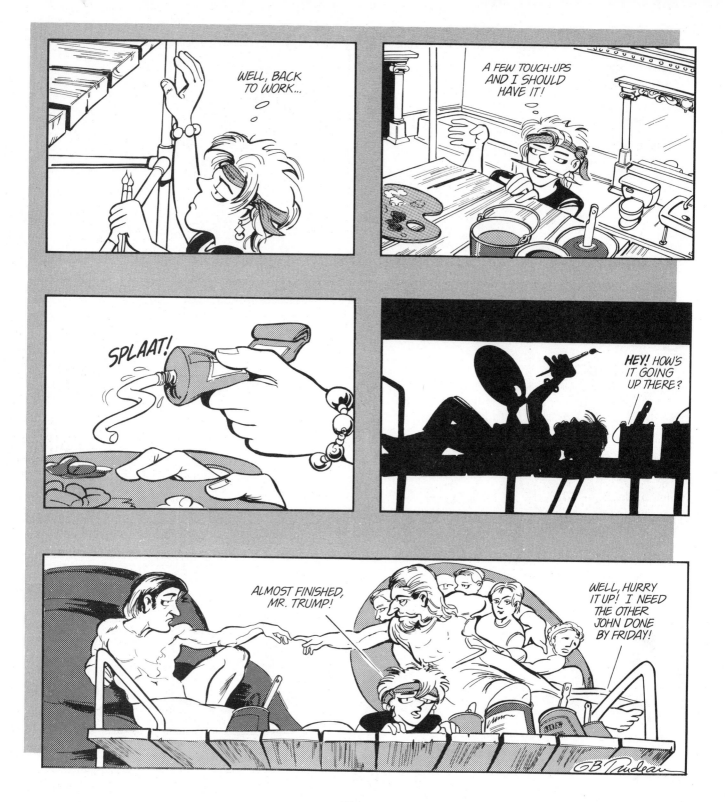

58

85

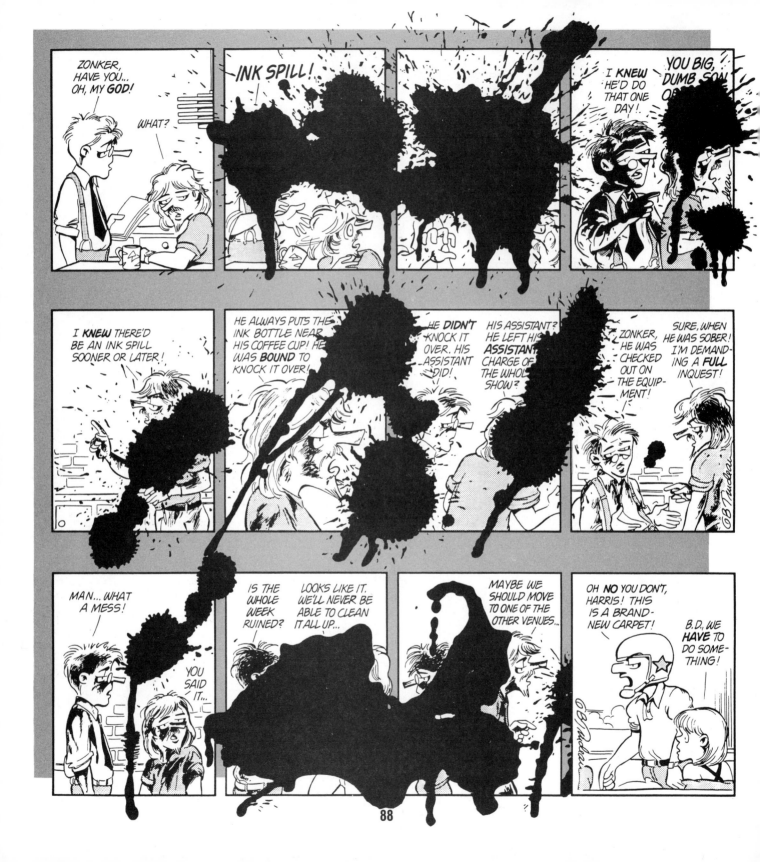